PAINTING THE TRUTH OF LIES

PAINTING THE TRUTH OF LIES

POEMS ON ART

ANN HOLMES

in memory of Sylvia Clark

ACKNOWLEDGMENTS

Thanks to Shaun Seymour and Stefan Petrmichl for their computer assistance, help formatting the book, and graphic design work on the cover.

To my sister, Jane Mason, with whom I first learned to love art

Thanks to my daughter, Megan Holmes, for proofreading this manuscript.

I am grateful to Sylvia Clark, Zdena Heller, John Meneghini, Jason Brown, and Aimee Weis for their support.

To my past editors, 2004, Ralph Nazareth, for *Shards*, Turn of the River Press and to iUniverse for *A Leaf Called Socrates*, 2011 *Play of Mirrors* 2016, *Alzheimer's Chronicles: When the Past is Not Present*, 2018.

We don't see things as they are
we see them as we are.
-Anais Nin

Other books by Ann Holmes:

Shards, Mashiko Poetry, Turn of River Press (2004)
A LEAF CALLED SOCRATES, iUniverse (2011)
A Play of Mirrors, iUniverse (2016)
Alzheimer's Chronicles: When The Past Is Not Present, iUniverse (2017)
A Glance Back, Poetry Memoire, iUniverse (2021)

INTRODUCTION

I had so many poems on art and artists over the years in my poetry collections and I dreamed of assembling them together in a single book. During the Covid-19 pandemic I had the opportunity to do this. Some of these poems are based on art that I saw in museums and on site, while others are about my own paintings made after the works of other artists. The poems create my own imaginary museum where I can live with these paintings every day.

POEMS

THE GARDEN OF EARTHLY DELIGHTS

THE GARDEN VANISHES	2
BEFORE TIME WAS TIME	3
AFTER THE FALL	4
THE GARDEN OF EARTHLY DELIGHTS	6
IF ONLY I'D BEEN THERE THEN	8
ARTICHOKES	9
FIRING MY MUSE	10
WILL VENUS RISE?	12
SURROUNDED BY UNFINISHED WOMEN	13
POLIO	14
FAMILY PORTRAIT	15
WHEN TOO MUCH IS NOT ENOUGH	16

HOW I BECAME A FAYUM MUMMY

TRAVELING GLASS	18
THE WAY	19
HOW I BECAME A FAYUM MUMMY	20
KEY TO TIME	22

TOURING THE RUINS

LEONARDO	24
LIFE CHANGES	25
SEPIA ANCESTORS	26
REVETMENT	27
DELPHI STILL LIFE	28

ROADSIDE SHRINE — 29
CUMAEAN SYBIL — 30
TOURING THE RUINS — 31
MEDUSA — 32

A SLICE OF MOONLIGHT

RED TAILED HAWK — 36
DEAD SWAN — 37
A LEAF CALLED SOCRATES — 38
NEAR AND CLOSE — 39
VISITOR — 40
THE GIRL IN A TREE — 41
HOPPER'S ROOM BY THE SEA — 42
WITHOUT — 43
THAT BITCH — 44
A SLICE OF MOONLIGHT — 45
CHINESE SCROLL — 46

A PLAY OF MIRRORS

LEAVING SAN CRESCI — 48
A PLAY OF MIRRORS — 49
TAG SALE CAMEO — 50

CHASTISEMENT OF LOVE

BEFORE MOCA OPENED — 52
GIVERNY — 53
FIRST LOVE — 54
LE DÉJEUNER SUR L'HERBE — 55

SELF-SEEKER	56
CHASTISEMENT OF LOVE	57

PAINTING THE TRUTH OF LIES

WHO SAYS THIS IS NOT A REMBRANDT?	60
DENYING THUMBS	61
PICASSO'S GUERNICA	63
YOU OWN A PAUL WIEGHARDT?	64
MEETING CHUCK CLOSE	65
ALICE NEEL AT SEVENTY-SEVEN	66
PAINTING THE TRUTH OF LIES	67
NOT FOGGED IN AT GAY HEAD	68

POETRY BONES

POETRY BONES	70
DISTRACTION	71
SPRING BEGINNING	72
WRAPPED IN LEAVES	74

MASHIKO

RIGHT WRONG ROAD	76
MY NEW ROOM	77
RED? NOT YET	78
SA MYO JI TEMPLE	79
RELIQUARY	80
TEN YEARS OF TEA CUPS	81
THE THREAT OF IMMORTALITY	82
COFFEE CEREMONY	83
NO GOOD AT WORDS	84

PATINA	85

THAT THAT CANNOT BE SEEN

THAT THAT CANNOT BE SEEN	88
COMPO BEACH	89
NETSUKE	90
SO LITTLE TIME	91
UNMOORED	92
NOTES	94
APPENDIX	99

THE GARDEN OF EARTHLY DELIGHTS

THE GARDEN VANISHES

She drinks
morning dew
f r o m   h i s
thigh. Leaves
rustle as
the Ser-
pent
glides
branch
to branch
r o u n d
that tree,
Its forked
tongue flicks
a parody of love.
That Apple shines,
round & red & ripe.
Falls into her hand.
He bites its glossy
skin, tart but not
unsweet. His lips
g r a z e   h e r
b r e a s t s.
Fingers
interlock.
T h e
Garden
vanishes.

BEFORE TIME WAS TIMED

Imagine when

mosquitoes, gnats,

wasps and bees

did not sting,

when all

Eve and Adam

did each day

was to bask

in the sunlight

and water

God's Garden,

Who'd expect God

to evict them

for one lousy apple?

AFTER THE FALL

When Eve mistook the serpent's hiss
for a servile smile and plucked That Apple
off That Tree, Eve barely had time to snatch
two fig leaves before God slammed shut
the Golden Gate, casting Eve and Adam
out of The Garden forever.

Because it is not recorded elsewhere,
I will tell what came next. Adam
had to invent new words:
Don't! Be careful!

Eve found them a cave with a splendid
lake view. Got rid of spiders and snakes
and swept out the bat-droppings.

Adam gathered rocks,
igneous and metamorphic,
to hurl at the dinosaurs.

So adorable were Cain and Able,
Eve almost forgot the pain
of birthing them.

Adam wove them a cradle
out of swamp grass and willow,
and Eve sang them this lullaby:

when the bough breaks,
down will come Cain
and Abel, with nary a scratch.

THE GARDEN OF EARTHLY DELIGHTS

Casals plays a Bach Suite on CD.
The phone rings. It is my friend.
She moved out. Has no time to talk.

Adam and Eve fidget
on their easel. I stare out of
my studio window,

no longer confident
of earth beneath the
ice-encrusted snow.

A hawk lands on a branch,
nearly close enough
to touch. Amber eyes blink

back my startled gaze.
The hawk sleeks its feathers,
folds its wings, as if posing

for Brancusi. Casals
hums louder
than his cello.

The Hawk flies off.
I glaze a translucent bubble
around Adam and Eve

so they might linger
a little longer
in The Garden.

After Hieronymus Bosch, *The Garden of Earthly Delights*
Prado, Madrid (painted by Ann Homes, 20 x 47 1/2")

IF ONLY I'D BEEN THERE THEN

I'd make everyone strip for Manet's *Déjeuner sur l'herbe*.
Play follow the dots with SEURAT.
Crash RENOIR's Boating Party.
Pose without an adorable child for MARY CASSATT.
Chill out with MONET'S *Water Lilies*.
Say, *enough already* to CEZANNE-
when painting *Mt. Sainte Victoire*.
Try to tell a cubist Picasso from a cubist Braque.
Buy a VAN GOGH before anyone else does.
Pirouette backstage with a DEGAS' dancer.
Weep with RODIN's *Burghers of Calais*.
Serve Coca-Cola to LAUTREC's Absinth Drinker.
Cure leprosy before GAUGUIN leaves for Tahiti.
Pull out the plug from Madame BONNARD'S bathtub.
Sharpen scissors for MATISSE'S cut-outs.
Find CAILLEBOTTE smaller umbrellas.
Enroll BOTERO's models at Weight Watchers.
Believe MAGRITTE when he says, *this is Not a pipe*.

ARTICHOKES

Yes, I heard the timer ding

but I was tweaking words.

Reluctantly, I break away

and take the artichokes

off the stove.

Back inside my poem

I flip background

to foreground,

tip my point of view

from me to you,

brush *sfumato* thoughts

with *chiaroscuro* light and dark

and scoop out its heart.

FIRING MY MUSE

My Muse is beautiful. Who would've
thought her Catherine Deneuve
with worry wrinkles that drip dry
and a benevolent evil eye?

Her lizard heels pinch my feet.
She's always in the judgment seat,
saying, simplify, clarify.
Her juicy syntax drains me dry.

Her thoughts are mine—mine hers.
The boundary between us blurs,
my anima and her animus
spiral a caduceus.

But who wants a two-headed snake?
Time to make a break,
shed our skins and divorce,
but would I feel remorse?

Would I write badly,
gladly or sadly?
Back off Bitch!
Bitch! Bitch! echoes

her doggerel prose.
Which of us is which?
Stay out of my context,
my Velcro subtext.

You ought to be seen!
You deserve a larger screen.
Her vanity I captivate,
her *muse-ship* she abdicates.

WILL VENUS RISE?

A Delft vase swings from a rope.
Botticelli grabs it. Turns it into
a *piñata* I whack with a #2 brush.
Blue and white shards shatter by my feet.
Out drop two Daumier magistrates,
who bow and doff top hats like the Cat
in a Hat. The one with the spectacles hands me
the Mary-half of a Fra Angelico Annunciation.
Mary, Mary, quite contrary.
I skateboard back to my easel where ideas
arrive in installments. (I am on sabbatical
from content.) But where did
Venus di Milo run off to?

After Botticelli, *Birth of Venus*, circa 1480, Uffizi, Florence
(painted by Ann Holmes, 15 1/2 x 19 1/2")

SURROUNDED BY UNFINISHED WOMEN

I model a terra cotta muse,
or does she model me?
She refuses to solidify.
Elusive, she
slips away.

I punch and gouge the clay.
Add and take away.
The muse plays hide and seek.
Reclusive, she
slips away.

I pound her a heart.
Hide it in her breast,
massage it until the beat is mine.
Intrusive, I
slip away.

POLIO

Reading Rita Dove's poem,
A Father Out Walking on the Lawn,
makes me think of my father
who walked only on city pavements.

During the sweltering Chicago summers,
my father wouldn't allow me to go
anywhere where crowds might be.

Not to the Art Institute
where in *Sunday Afternoon in the Park*,
I could no longer take that monkey
for a walk, and instead,

cooled by the measured draft
of a revolving fan, I spent
each afternoon in bed,
reading Oz books, dressing
and undressing paper dolls,
and still, I got polio.

FAMILY PORTRAIT

The ruffles on Auntie Park's bonnet
date her to the late nineteenth century.

The family claims her as the first
woman slum-landlord in St. Louis.
Her smile appears unpracticed,
perhaps tacked on by a limner artist
to make her appear friendly.

One night Auntie Park leapt off
the dining room wall, splattering bits
of gold-chipped frame everywhere.

Her latest trick is to turn on the *Bose*
at any hour of the night. If only

she'd turn down the volume,
we wouldn't mind a little
late night music.

Amanda Maria Morgan
("Auntie Park"), possibly by
George Caleb Bingham
(1811-1897)

WHEN TOO MUCH IS NOT ENOUGH

Imagine being in New York, seeing art
every day until there is no more art left
to see. Where to start?

At the Met, MoMA, the Guggenheim,
the Frick, the Whitney, the Cloisters,
the Neue, the Morgan, the Japan House,
the Onassis, Noguchi or Asia House?

This was before Covid-19 and now
Omicron, when too much art
became no art left to see, aside
from the art inside books,
magazines and TV.

HOW I BECAME A FAYUM MUMMY

TRAVELING GLASS

On my way

to Yokohama,

I squeeze onto

a jammed-packed

train, see a self

not myself

mirrored in the

window pane,

cheek bones widen,

eyes aslant as I try

to peel off my

western mask.

THE WAY

An arcane sect of monks wearing night goggles
and putty-colored cloaks come toward me.
I step aside, as I would for a herd of goats.
Their chants echo off the polygonal walls.
An elder tugs at my sleeve. *Follow us or you
lose the way. (What way?)* I follow their
non-stop fugues across a bridge, over
a riverbed made of crazed earth. I climb
sedimentary cliffs, strewn with human bones,
famine and plague. The rosy dawn unveils
the rubble from the Tower of Babel. The monks
squat on rocks. Unlace their sandals. Shake
out the grit. An elder hands me
a putty-colored cloak and a spare
pair of night goggles.

HOW I BECAME A FAYUM MUMMY

I've come to paint your portrait,
says a man tapping at
my window pane. *Why?* I ask.
*Because Isis wants to know
what you look like.*
*Why should Isis give a fig
what I look like?*
    achoo

I grab a hanky out of
a fold of my *chiton*.
to blow my nose.

*Why not come next week
when my cold is gone?*
    achoo

He shakes his head no.
Drops white pigment
on his pallet to match
the pallor of my face.

I fall sound asleep. Wake just as
the painter is packing up his paints.

Now I get it! The painted me
is my picture ID
to let Isis know

it is me he is to lead
on the treacherous journey
into the afterlife.

My painted self stares
back at me, looking
pretty chipper
for someone dying.

After an ancient Egyptian Fayum portrait
Detroit Institute of Art
(painted by Ann Holmes, 12 x 9")

KEY TO TIME

I lift the lid off a red suede box,
shoved behind the desk drawer.
Don't, warns Mother. (From time
to time, she makes a guest appearance
in a dream.) Inside the box is a jade necklace.
Its string snaps. Beads recoil, perhaps
offended by the warmth of my hand. Bounce
on the floor. Turn into mice and scurry off.
The key, the key, Mother cries. Wedged
into the lid of the box is the burnished
Key to Time. I fit it into the grandmother
clock no one remembers to set.
Try to nudge time a moment forward,
a moment back, but time will not budge.

TOURING THE RUINS

LEONARDO

I leap out of bed, past
that inscrutable
smile of Mona Lisa's,

to my blueprints
that will fly us higher
than birds, higher
than clouds.

What a harebrained idea,
even for the most
sophisticated enlightened
Renaissance mind to contemplate?

Odder than melting glaciers
and the greenhouse effect
of global warming.

After Leonardo da Vinci, *Mona Lisa*
Louvre, Paris
(painted by Ann Holmes, 19 x 16").

LIFE CHANGES

Last time we went to Tanglewood
we stayed at our favorite Lennox guest house,
the one with nine cats. (Was it Mendelssohn
Joshua Bell played?)

That was when we thought we'd live
on the east coast forever, we'd live
in the same house forever,
that we'd live forever.

Whenever we felt like it, we'd hop
on *Metro North*. See a play,
Go to the Met, Guggenheim, MoMA,
the Frick or Whitney.

That was when *he* stopped
taking books out of the library, stopped
weeding the garden, stopped
remembering who called.

That was when I began to sift
through things.
Did I own them,
or did they own me?

SEPIA ANCESTORS

Garbage day in Erytrea.
Blue plastic bags line the curbs.
A sepia photograph of *Yaya*
with her six mustached sons
lean on a yellow basket,
the frame askew,
        glass cracked.

When *Yaya* birthed
son after son, behind
the curtained door
did she forget to hang
the blue-eyed charm
to deceive
        the evil eye?

Six dressed in their
Sunday best,
hair trimmed,
handkerchiefs poke
out of jacket pockets,
mud from artichoke fields
cling to shoes, scuffed
        past polishing.

I load *Yaya* with her six sons,
into my hatchback. Since
they posed for this portrait,
I doubt they strayed
more than a donkey ride
        from home.

REVETMENT

A three-legged tourist, fresh
from the riddle of the sphinx, clacks
up the white marble stairway
of the Athens Byzantine Museum.

I follow the tkk-tkk-tkk of his walking stick
into a roomful of silver-covered icons.
What are these? he asks.
The two of us are the only ones
in the museum.

Revetment, I say—a name
I read aloud off a label,
pinned to the wall.

They are icons of Mary,
Jesus and the saints. the Greeks kiss
when they pray. Silver protects
the paint from sticky fingers and kissing lips.

The tourist laughs. *Kiddo, I betcha*
five euros, nothing is underneath.
Why paint what no one will sees?

Outside a sudden gust of wind whips
strands of silver hair across my face.

DELPHI STILL LIFE

On the way to Delphi,
our guide points out the crossroad
where Oedipus murdered his father
as if it had really happened.

Weeds sprout out of the Sybil's rock,
fallen from the Phaedriades.
I stand where she stood,
predicting the Trojan War.

The theater is roped off after
two thousand years of feet.
I cannot skip tier to tier,
or pretend to hear
Aeschylus and Sophocles.

Here's the mountain Aesop
climbed, enemies at his heels.
Despite the clever fox he was,
they pushed him off the cliff.

On a marble *metope*
along The Sacred Way,
a goddess rides sidesaddle
with half-a-head, half-a-smile.

A headless god spears
a skirted goddess, limbs askew,
as if bodies were walls
to break through.

ROADSIDE SHRINE

Birds too far away
to identify, bound
for a bird-task, where
will they alight?

A shrine on stilts marks
where a wingless car
flew off the road.

I unlatch the glass door.
to a Byzantine saint,
torn from a book.

A wick floats
in a jam-jar
of olive oil.

I strike a match
Is it dark enough
to light the flame?

CUMAEAN SYBIL

The cave air chills my arms.
Our guide, Eugenia, identifies
where the Cumaean Sybil fasted,

chewed on laurel leaves,
shouted out oracles,
even foretold
the birth of Christ.

Wild dogs dart
from a patch of shade
to a patch of sunlight.

Eugenia fingers her
sun-bleached hair,
directs our gaze to a pile

of rocks, formerly
a temple to Jupiter,
later converted
to a Christian basilica,

now a pile of rubble
for the Cumaean dogs
to squat over.

TOURING THE RUINS

I follow Christina's graceful sandaled feet
over Cretan rubble. She points at
a squared-off rock where ancient
potters made pots.

Digital cameras flash.

I pick up a shard from the lip
of a wide-mouthed jar. Slip it
into my pocket.

Christina leads us to still
another pile of rubble. This one
blocks a passage to the underworld.

Digital cameras flash.

I sit on what I suspect is no ordinary rock.
Shake out the pebbles from my sock.

MEDUSA

Asleep on my granite bed, I dream
    I turn the whole world into stone.
    Wake with a smile,

Comb my snakes into a crown.
    Perseus sees me mirrored
    in Athena's shield.

I don't see him, cloaked
    in his invisibility. With
    a diamond sword,

he wipes my smile.
    Clips Hermes' winged-slippers
    onto his heels. Flings my head

into a gunnysack. Soars
    above a sea I cannot see:
    Ionian? Aegean?

Perseus swoops down to rescue
    Andromeda, chained
    onto a rock, about

to be devoured
    by a ravenous serpent,
    although serpents

I know are vegetarian.
    Perseus slays
    the serpent,

frees Andromeda, flees
    to an island west of east—
    Cycladic? Dodecanese?

He removes my severed head.
    Trees and a well
    are all I see.

Dangles my head
    over the well water.
    I flash him a beguiling smile.

Splash him with my rhinestone tears.
    Perseus cries, *look, Andromeda,*
    how beautiful Medusa is!

Dutiful, Andromeda looks.
    Perseus kisses lips
    she cannot lift

in a smile.
    I turn her heart
    to alabaster.

After Edward Burne-Jones, *The Baleful Head*, from the Perseus Series, Staatsgalerie, Stuttgart (painted by Ann Holmes, 24.5 X 24.5")

A SLICE OF MOONLIGHT

RED-TAILED HAWK

The New York Times is not
in our driveway. The snow plow
hasn't come yet to dig us out.
I stare at the junco pecking at seed,
spilled by a drab-colored finch
glued at the feeder. (By April,
it will turn a dazzling yellow.)
 A red-tailed hawk swoops
off a page of my Audubon book.
Grabs the finch right off the feeder
I wish I hadn't remembered
to fill. I didn't mean to
set the scene for a winter kill.

DEAD SWAN

No wound visible.
No clue why it died.

The poet lifts a wing.
Wing span as
wide as he is tall.

The poet reads at a gallery
of black and white
photography.

Two women dressed
in pastel pant suits
squeeze between

a fence and barn, trample
the dead swan.
The poet predicts

scavengers will come
to pick the carcass clean.

I welcome the two intruders
They delay its decay.

A LEAF CALLED SOCRATES
In memory of Marion and Albert Hubbell

Albert paints Marion
a rose, white
in the morning sunlight.

A wise old leaf
Marian names Socrates
hovers between

the window and the screen,
along with a white feather
she calls Snow Queen.

A sunflower grows
from a seed she
tosses to the crows.

Bows its head to
the scavengers she feeds.

NEAR AND CLOSE
      In memory of Marion Hubbell

In last night's dream
Marion's ghost instructs
me to go online
and google
NEAR and CLOSE.

Marion once met a ghost
in an antique shop.
It snatched the plate
right out of her hands
and smashed it on the floor.

When I wake I google *NEAR* and *CLOSE*:
about to happen, involving regular contact,
allowing little space between.

For the life of me, I can't imagine
what is *ABOUT TO HAPPEN*
between me alive
and *Marion dead.*

VISITOR
In memory of Marion Hubbell

Remember	Though
when Jesus	you didn't
barged into	quite
your shower	believe
stall and	in him,
with his	you did
unblessing	open
hand he	the
wiped away	shower
your tears?	door.

GIRL IN A TREE
   In memory of Jane Flanders

It is late October, cold enough
to button up your sweater.

The sunflower that seeded itself
in your bed of beans now withers.
Your inside plants cannot fathom
why your outside plants lose leaves.

If you do not climb down,
then I will climb up.

I pluck out sticks and leaves caught
in your curly white hair. Soon as these
trees become bare, you will be lifeless.

HOPPER'S ROOM BY THE SEA
In memory of Pete Stout

A woman yells

into her cell phone

to someone

not nearly as far

away as you.

I see you in Hopper's room

by the sea where sunlight

angles onto sea-blue walls.

Don't worry

Death takes time

to get used to.

WITHOUT

I cannot imagine
Eavan Boland without
magenta swerves;

W.S. Merwin without
a diffident music; Emily
Dickinson without *her*
dissonant message.

I can live without
a Roman lacrimatory:
a tear shaped flask
that traps the spill
of an eye.

The truth is
I don't own one,
but I read about it
in yesterday's

New York Times,
and now I can't live
without the idea.

THAT BITCH

my Muse

absconded

with a fistful

of my words.

What if I

scribble

a sonnet

to an ocelot,

take up chess

like Duchamp did,

once his nude

finally made it

down the stairs.

A SLICE OF MOONLIGHT

enters my
　bedroom
　　window,
　　　bright
　　　　enough
　　　　　to inspect
　　　　　　the pale
　　　　　　　skin on
　　　　　　　　the inside
　　　　　　　　　of my left
　　　　　　　　　　forearm
　　　　　　　　　　for the
　　　　　　　　　　　indelible
　　　　　　　　　　　　stain of
　　　　　　　　　　　　　invisible
　　　　　　　　　　　　　　numbers.

CHINESE SCROLL

Evening mist blurs
brush strokes on
twisted pine

so I nearly miss
the inch-high
naked monk,

bent over
the steep
mountain path,

scarcely care
if he ever
reaches

the tea hut,
perched

so precipitously.
on a rock.

A PLAY OF MIRRORS

LEAVING SAN CRESCI
    to Megan and Lia

Once this room stored wine and oil,
maybe even goats and chickens. Now the
walls are plastered with hand swirls.
The linen on the bed, time-yellowed.

Reflected in the mirror is half
a marriage portrait.
Is it your landlady's
or someone
bought?

I leave the door ajar. Thunder
stumbles over mountains.
Apennine applause
for my ten days here.

Beneath sliced tree crossbeams,
unglazed tiles take on the flesh tones
of Lia's baby body. The mirror mirrors
no one. Whoever she was, gone to glass.

A PLAY OF MIRRORS

I look past
the me
I was
to the me
I have become.

I used to urge
my father to be grateful
for what he still could do,
sanctimonious fool I was.

How I miss crossing
the flowered courtyard
at the Frick, making a beeline
for Ingres' *Comtesse d'Haussonville*,
in her lavender taffeta gown.

I used to stare at her and I *swear*
she stared back at me,
each of us both the viewer
and the viewed.

TAG SALE CAMEO

Nothing is truly mine except my name
                    Stanley Kunititz

Rummaging through a Ferragamo shoe box
of junk jewelry, I spot a cameo, a classic profile
of a girl with a ponytail. It reminds me of the cameos,
pinned on boards outside tourist shops in Sorrento.
I paid a dollar to a woman in shorts and a halter. In no way
does this new tag sale cameo resemble my sister's
Pre-Raphaelite cameo, stolen by burglars
her neighbors, sipping vodka tonics, thought
were there to mow the lawn.

CHASTISEMENT OF LOVE

BEFORE MOCA OPENED
Museum of contemporary art, North Adams, MA.

The Guard, Ed, shows me the half moon burnt
into floor boards where mama once sat
at Sprague Electric, Building 4,
rolling capacitors. Mama stuffed
cotton in her ears not to hear
grinding and grating.

Before MoCa opened to the public,
guards were given a crash-course
on modern art.

Some tell Ed they prefer hearing
him more than professional guides.

Upstairs I hear footsteps
of visitors looking at
Anslem Kiefer's *Seasons*.

It's quiet except for
creaking floorboards.

GIVERNY

My dream-door opens

to a triptych

of Monet waterlilies.

Hitler wades in.

Monet's water lilies

don't like being jostled.

Has my dream-assassin

come to murder

one more Jew?

FIRST LOVE
After Caravaggio's *Cupid*

I was eleven. Love

an angel just my age,

flesh silk, penis smiling

like his lips. Scattered

by Love's feet

were a violin, bow,

musical score, and a nail

from the Cross, symbols

unknown to me then when

I gazed on Love with the craving

that grafts a woman onto a girl.

DEJOURNER SUR L'HERBE
After Eduard Manet's *Luncheon on the Grass*

One Sunday, I sneak up on Manet's *Luncheon
on the Grass*, curious what they had to say.
The three sit on a blanket. Babette
peels foil off foie gras and camembert.
Andre passes a bottle of pinot noir. Stefan
tears open a baguette. Andre suggests *Babette
take off her fucking frock*. She laughs, why not?
Wiggles her bare toes in morning dew. Andre
wonders aloud why neither he nor Stefan
got into the this year's *Salon de Refuses*.
A woman dressed in a filmy toga beckons Babette
to come over. Braids sprigs of clover
into Babette's wavy brown hair. The two
lie on the sun-warmed grass.

SELF-SEEKER

My art is like
the mocking
bird's song.

I borrow Narcissus
from Boltraffio.

Paint him
in a weeping cave.

His pond is
my stream.

Where is my reflection?
Where is my reflection?

After Giovanni Antonio Boltraffio, *Narcissus*, Uffizi, Florence
(painted by Ann Holmes, 15 1/2 x 19 1/2")

CHASTISEMENT OF LOVE
After Manfredi's *Chastisement of Love*

At ten I fell madly in love
with the *Chastisement of Love*,
then when everyone thought
painted by Caravaggio,
but later reattributed
to Manfredi, a follower
of Caravaggio

The question is why
ten-year-old me
was obsessed
by this winged boy
being viciously attacked?

I used to stare at the silken flesh tones,
passionate reds, smoky umber,
colors oozing like honey off the pallet.

I did not focus on anything:
not the angel, assailant,
or the woman trying
to intervene.

I was caught up in a crescendo
of brutality, vulnerability and
helplessness.

At least I didn't grow up
to be a sadomasochist.

PAINTING THE TRUTH OF LIES

WHO SAYS THIS IS NOT A REMBRANDT?
    After Rembrandts(?)*Polish Rider*

The Polish Rider is about to gallop out
of the Grand Gallery
of the Frick.

Even I know The Polish Rider
in the red tights on the white horse
is Rembrandt's son, Titus.

While the Rembrandt Research Project concedes
that The Polish Rider was begun by Rembrandt,
the credit is his who wields the last stroke.

Rembrandt aficionados took years
to scrutinize every so-called Rembrandt
in the museums throughout the world.

But what if there's only a hair's difference
if it is or is not a Rembrandt?
Will someone on the committee
spend the night in a sweat?

The Polish Rider is about to be deaccessioned,
when the Frick curators shout, *NO!*

Titus pivots the white horse back
to the empty space where he belongs.

DENYING THUMBS

When *the Denial of St. Peter* was new at the Met,
I tried painting an appropriation of it at home.

My sole source of light comes from the moon
Caravaggio did not paint.
This leaves me in the dark,
painting another painter's painting.

A Roman centurion aims
a gloved index finger at St. Peter,
who would, if he could, back right
out of the picture plane.

By him stands a hazel-eyed woman,
who, with both hands,
points at St. Peter.

My brush delights in painting
stripes of moonlight ricocheting
off crinkles in her scarf.

The last thing I paint
is St. Peter's denying thumbs:
    Not me!
       Not me!
          Not me!

After Caravaggio, *The Denial of St. Peter*
Metropolitan Museum of Art, New York
(painted by Ann Holmes, 25 x 31 1/2")

PICASSO'S GUERNICA

Everything I know about the Spanish Civil War comes
from reading Hemmingway and Picasso's *Guernica*.
The backless oak bench where I used to sit, staring at *Guernica*
at MOMA was barely long enough for four strangers to share.
The dead child held stiffly in its mother's arms
reminds me of an ancient temple offering.
A male corpse lies spread eagle on the ground.
A woman thrusts a lighted candle out her window,
as if it might shed light on the horror happening.
A stylized horse gallops nowhere. I recognize
a Picasso bull next to the woman with the dead child.
but I couldn't figure out why Picasso painted
an electric light bulb where the sun should be.

YOU OWN A PAUL WIEGHARDT?

exclaimed a new friend when I opened
my door. She is the first one
to recognize Paul's painting.

A man suspended in a red geometric space,
hovers over a turquoise typewriter.

A woman in a lime-green tunic,
combs her lithe fingers through a cascade
of auburn hair. My parents bought this painting
and now it is mine. It was the first
painting Paul sold in Chicago.

Paul applied old masters' under-painting
techniques for the skin tones.

Shhh--don't wake that tabby cat
asleep on the checkered couch.

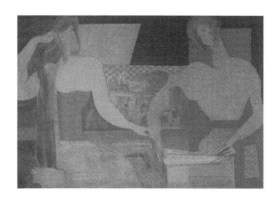

Paul Wieghardt, Untitled,
in the collection of Ann Holmes
(43 x 60")

MEETING CHUCK CLOSE
    New York, 1979

I almost met Chuck Close at the Pace Gallery,
when he was exhibiting his gigantic heads.
I say "almost" met him because
I never actually did see him.

He spoke, hidden behind
a pot of large yellow lilies
from inside the gallery's office.

Some one from where I was standing,
asked whether he took commissions?

*No! Something has to be radically wrong with you
if you want a nine foot portrait of yourself.*

*Don't you get bored, painting
the same face for fourteen months?*

*Don't you get bored going to the same office, day after day,
doing the same thing day, after day?
Sure I get bored.*

ALICE NEEL AT SEVENTY-SEVEN
    New York, 1980

The day I met Alice Neel at her Madison Avenue gallery,
she looked squinty-eyed at my sister and me. (Was
she imagining us without clothes.)

I stare at a wall of nudes: daughter-in-law,
about to give birth to twins, the art critic,
Cindy Nemser sitting nude on a couch with her boyfriend;
Andy Warhol's nude bandaged body, riddled
with bullet holes; Joe Gould, nude, with a triple-penis.

Alice tells us she did everything here in a single year.

Adding, apparently out of nowhere,
in America a rose is not a rose.
It is a CHEAP rose
or an EXPENSIVE rose.

What would Gertrude Stein
have said about Alice Neel's rose
with a price tag?

PAINTING THE TRUTH OF LIES
After Beckmann's *The Actors*

Beckmann was witness to a shameful age,
the world his triptych, a painted stage.
He depicted the rage of Europe,
a sideshow of musicians, crooks and spies.
Two-faced Janus, blind on a pedestal.
A king with a feathered cloak stabs
himself in the heart. (Is his bloody
dagger real or a prop?) On the steps,
off to one side, a man scans the headlines
of *the New York Times*. Beside him lies
a pair of shackled ankles and bare feet.
A woman with an unfocused gaze holds up
a mirror to her deadpan face, trying
to approximate the calm of an altarpiece.

NOT FOGGED IN AT GAY HEAD
   (Gay Head, Martha's Vineyard, Massachusetts)

We follow less
than perfect nudes

up a cliff. Wait
our turn. Slip

into a pool
of hot bubbling clay.

I slather you with liquid-earth.
Easy as icing a cake. Camouflaged

as George Segal statues,
we splash into the ocean.

Rinse the glaze of anonymity
off shivering bodies.

POETRY BONES

POETRY BONES

All I know is I am leading thirty-seven poets,
vagrants, penitents, wandering from
fiefdom to fiefdom, searching for poetry
bones. I don't know why they are thirty-
seven—not three and seven—or why *I* am
in charge—nothing you'd catch me at
awake. I don't know if these thirty-seven,
with their middle aged patina, took a wrong
turn into my dream, where as far as I know,
no poetry bones are buried. I don't even know
what poetry bones are, what they'd look like,
what to do were I to find them? Call in an
archaeologist? Erect a shrine? Throw
the *I Ching*? Flesh them into a poem?

DISTRACTION
In Memory of Gita Peshko

I dream I am in a garden with my friend. Gita.
Surprise! she shouts, slipping
a necklace of crystallized
tears over my head.

Gita's gifts
were always exquisite,
bought for the me
she wished me to be.

As she's about to speak,
a faun ambles into my dream.
Licks my cheek. I shoo it away.

Glance at the empty
nearness where
Gita used to be.

SPRING BEGINNING
In Memory of Gita Peschko

I want to show you
spring beginning,
even here on city streets.

Where are we by the way?
Good to locate poems
and dreams.

See these trees?
I grew up with city trees:
stunted buds
on knotted twigs.

Here, look through my eyes
at the spring caterpillar flowers
that splatter Chicago sidewalks
and stain my shoes red.

See the cherry blossoms?
I prefer them weeping.

I follow the cherry blossoms
on your kimono upstairs
into a roomful of clouds
by The Cloud Master.

I pick up the phone
to hear your voice.
It is someone else.

You have no voice.
Your body's hills
and valleys are
winter still.

Beyond your vanishing
point, do you see
spring beginning?

WRAPPED IN LEAVES
In Memory of Gita Peshko

We escape where no escape seems possible.
Leaves shield us. Your leaf-green *sari* acts
as camouflage. You lead me into an unnamed city.
Katmandu? Remember poinsettias,
red as Christmas?

Rocks strapped onto young boys' foreheads as they
climb to a shrine. *Like Sisyphus,* you might have said.
Red and yellow leaves push against the picture plane,
spill out the frame. *Like a Mannerist painting,*
yoou might have said.

You and I gather leaves, but not as fast as they fall.
I paste them on with spit. You grab a paint brush.
Chlorophyll them green. I position my hands,
finger to finger, thumb to thumb.

form an Islamic arch. You step between
my finger-frame. Your vines entwine
my knuckles. Wrapped
in leaves, you leave.

MASHIKO
A Pottery Village in Japan

RIGHT WRONG ROAD

Lost, Yukako swerves. Skids.
Front wheels spin in air.
A potter runs over. Finds
two neighbors. They
lift the car out of the mud.
and he invites us to tea.

Yukako jabs her thumb at me.
She's looking for a place to work.

I'm unskilled, I begin.
Yukako elbows me.
In Japanese, she means.

The potter is on his way to Chiba,
van stacked with pots. He lights
a cigarette. *She could work here*
he says.

MY NEW ROOM

We climb up stairs
with no downstairs,
a de Chirico painting,
suspended in air.

Beneath us is a woodshed,
stacked with firewood:
walls, ceilings and floors
of ramshackle houses.

I breathe in a scent
of freshly laid *tatami*.

A rooster crows.
A dog barks.

I look out the window
at a parody of the Japanese flag,
a red sunset in a white sky:

Yukako opens a door
to what I fear the most:
a squat-down in-door outhouse.

RED? NOT YET

Sensei bows. He whispers a prayer to
the fire gods. Lights the flame.
Scrimmed in smoke, Emi on her pogo stick,
fades and reappears. A professional firer,
Minagawa, comes to help with the firing.
Tall and thin as a Giacometti sculpture,
chain-saws twelve foot planks into four foot
lengths. Tosses them left, center, right. He
guides my arm. My aim falls short. Humidity
slows the firing. *Sensei* shouts, *Watch out!*
and drives off. Watch out? What for? Fire
snaps. Chambers fume. Yumiko brings us
steaming noodles. Minagawa uncaps
a peep hole. Orange flames
leap out. *Red? Not yet.*
Sensei comes back. Minagawa
takes a break, long skinny legs
splay out over the ground.

SAIMYO-JI TEMPLE

Zodiac beasts
lick their lips
at oranges
on the altar.

Men wearing
leather shoes
fling straw sandals
onto trees.

I look into a room,
reluctant to admit
the light
of a four o'clock sky.

I see a demon, tall
as two of me, eyes
rolled back,

and sprawled
on the ground,
are the thousand

paper cranes
that failed to heal
a dying child.

Have I found
a dumping ground
for hope gone wrong?

RELIQUARY

Kiln-warm, Hamada's pots amble
down the path, as if strolling
down the Ginza in twos or threes.
Hamada inspects this bowl,
that pitcher, decorated in wax resist,
round rimmed spectacles, two
luminous moons, perched halfway
down his nose. I know Hamada
from stories potters tell, like when
he begged his dying kiln for one last firing.
Their glazes stunned everyone.

Once my fortune cookie said, *the onion
you are eating is some else's water lily*.
Today Hamada's field
by the big gate is paved
for tour busses. *Shoji* doors slide
open to an Eames chair, chests
and folkware from all over the world.
On the back wall is a black and white Hamada,
his expression quizzical. Bald head bent
over pots begging for his approval.

TEN YEARS OF TEACUPS
   Ken Murata

Hamada said, *make the same*
teacup again and again.
I didn't think I could. For ten years
I made teacups. Even now
to get the clay
used to my hands
I practice on the teacup

As sketching is for the artist,
the teacup is basic to know
and practice.

One day I asked Hamada if I had talent.
I remember him standing there, his arms
folded around my question.
He pointed to an old man, hunched
over a wheel, turning one
flawless vase after another.

We cannot match the skill
of this worker's many many
years. Your pottery is off balance:
too much of something,
too little of something else.
Form is proportion. Repeat
what you do now.

THREAT OF IMMORTALITY
   Sui Nagakura

We sip green tea from Nagakura's
green glazed cups. I pick up a bowl,
green as the stones I slipped on
on the way to her studio.
She grabs the bowl and holds it up,
as if it were a temple offering.

*Suppose I sold you this bowl today
and tomorrow, didn't like it,
wished it didn't exist.*

*This bowl I hate
might last
a thousand years.*

COFFEE CEREMONY

Yasuda slips a cord beneath a spinning cup.
Frees it from a cone of clay. Agitates coffee beans
over white hot coals. The fragrance masks
the scent of clay. Caught up in the ritual,
I watch the grinder spin
faster than the wheel. Simple gestures.
No word spoken to disrupt the shift
from art to life. Yasuda lifts
the kettle off the fire. Pours
water, on the verge of boiling,
through a store-bought filter.
The coffee steeps. An alchemy
of liquid amber. He hands me
a crackled celadon cup I raise
to my lips. Breathe in the elixir
of freshly ground coffee.

NO GOOD AT WORDS
   Shoji Kamota

When I read a book, I might
remember a sentence or two I like,
but I cannot sum up the plot.

Maybe this is true
for all Japanese.
Our culture is legless.

When I look at a Durer
the meaning is clear.

The Japanese brush
plays tricks. The meaning
gets lost. We call it,
pretending not to know.

We Japanese are silent
even as we speak.

PATINA
    Totaro Sukuma

Rooms once dark,
    fill with sunlight.
    Glass replaces
opaque screens

Once we sat on the floor
    on cushions.
    Now chairs raise
our point of view

At the wheel
    I think of the ways
    we see and use pottery.
These cups we drink from

were made by me
    thirty-five years ago.
    My pottery and I
grow old together.

Our touch
    softens the patina
    makes the glaze
more beautiful.

THAT THAT CANNOT BE SEEN

THAT THAT CANNOT BE SEEN

For fifteen hundred years,
two un-Islamic Buddhas
stood on a cliff in Bamiyan,
Afghanistan, until
the Taliban smashed
them to bits with TNT.

If these two Buddhas
were still in Bamiyan,
I'd never see them,

and yet I see that that
cannot be seen:
two Buddhas,
two towers.

COMPO BEACH

Waves wash away
my footprints
in wet sand.

I pick up a clam shell.
Good. It's empty.
The hermit crab
that once
lived inside
it is gone.

I too cast off
my former
artist selves.

Sand erases.
Time forgets.

NETSUKE

I wish you could slide your fingers
over my ivory Noh dancer, small
enough to cradle
in your hand, but you can't

because a dropout delinquent
hired to do house repairs, stole
him off my fireplace mantel.

My Noh dancer was two-faced:
When swiveled halfway
round, it turns into a devil.

Picture *his* netsuke in a devil mask,
inert on an unswept floor, strewn
with Styrofoam cups and rancid socks.

Freed from the clutch of his fingers,
it craves the touch of my palm.

SO LITTLE TIME

If I belong anywhere in Dante's Inferno,

it is where poets, artists, actors

and magicians are,

heads stitched on backwards

to ease the strain

of swiveling around

to focus on the past.

Please let me know,

if there is time left

to bone up on Dante?

UNMOORED

from sun, moon, stars,
sight, sound, touch,
laughter—yours and mine,
nothing left do I desire,

no   Bosch,
         Michelangelo
         Caravaggio

no   Van Gogh
         Matisse
         Picasso

no   Bach
         Beethoven
         Mozart

no   Shakespeare
         Blake
         T.S. Eliot,

Wait   please — I need
a little bit more time
to finish my poem.

NOTES

Epigraph, 1951, attributed to Anais Nin, also a Talmudic saying from the *Tamada Seduction of the Talmada* (University of Chicago Press, 1951).

6. THE GARDEN OF EARTHY DELIGHTS (1515), by Hieroymus Bosch, b. 1450 -d. 1516,, Prado, Madrid, Spain.

9. ARTICHOKES. Sfumato - soft smoky effects in Renaissance painting.

13. SURROUNDED BY UNFINISHED WOMEN. *Unfinished women* are made of clay.

15. FAMILY PORTRAIT. The portrait represents Amanda Marie Morgan Park, nicknamed Auntie Park. It is unsigned but possibly by George Bingham, who worked in Saint Louis in the 1920's-30's.

16. WHEN TOO MUCH IS NOT ENOUGH. About how the Delta variant of Covid-19 shut all the art museums and galleries.

18. TRAVELING GLASS. My first poem, written in the early 1970s, on the train to Yokohama, about how my looking into a warped window pane turned me into a Japanese.

20. HOW I BECAME A FAYUM MUMMY. Fayum mummy funerary portraits were among the earliest painted human likenesses. Artisans with paint and pallets visited the sick and dying to paint their portraits so Apollo or Isis or another god could recognize who they were to lead into the underworld.

22. *KEY TO TIME*. A dream.

24. *LEONARDO*. About how Leonardo believed humans would fly and I have him imagine global warming and the green house effect.

27. *REVETMENT*. Revetment is a metal covering to protect Byzantine devotional painting.

29. *ROADSIDE SHRINE*. Road shrines in Greece are erected on sites where a fatal accident occurred.

30. *CUMAEAN SYBIL*. The Cumaean Sybil presided over the Apollonian oracle at Cumae near Naples.

31. *TOURING THE RUINS*. Tourists taking photographs of nothing.

37. *DEAD SWAN*. A poetry reading in 2002, inspired by Eamon Grennan's poem, *Swan in Winter*, at Silvermine Gallery, New Canaan Ct.

38-40. *A LEAF CALLED SOCRATES, NEAR AND CLOSE and VISITOR*. Poems about Albert and Marion Hubbell.

41. *THE GIRL IN A TREE*. Jane Flanders, my first poetry instructor, who later died of cancer, wrote a poem by the same name.

42. *HOPPER'S ROOM BY THE SEA*, 1951, at Yale University Art Gallery.

43. *WITHOUT*. This poem references two contemporary poets, Evan Boland and W. S. Merwyn, with quotes from their work. Lacrimatory is defined within the poem.

48. *LEAVING SAN CRESCI*, town, north of Florence Italy.

49. *A PLAY OF MIRRORS. Countess d'Haussonville by George Ingres, 1846*, at the Frick Museum, New York.

55. *DEJOURNER SUR L'HERBE*. Acting out my fantasy about Manet's painting.

57. *CHASTISEMENT OF LOVE*. George de la Tour, Washington, National Gallery, 1493-1553, 71 x 44 1/2. A favorite painter of mine. When I decided to turn my home into a museum, George de la Tour, Bosh, and Caravaggio were the first artists I copied. Inspired by

Boltraffio, a follower of da Vinci's, I first learned how to paint drapery.

60. *WHO SAID THIS IS NOT A REMBRANDT?* The Rembrandt Research Project unsuccessfully tried to have the Frick Rembrandt decommissioned, but the curators at the Frick objected.

61. *DENYING THUMBS*. This painting represent St. Peter denying that he knew Jesus.

63. *PICASSO'S GUERNCA*, was moved to Spain in 1981.

64. *YOU OWN A PAUL WEIGHARDT?* Paul Weighardt's wife, Nelli, was a babysitter for my new friend when the Weighardts emigrated from Europe to Pittsfield, Massachusetts. I knew the Weighardts at the Art Institute of Chicago, where as a teenager, I studied sculpture with Paul's wife, Nelli.

67. *PAINTING THE TRUTH OF LIES*, is my title for Max Beckmen's painting "Actors" a triptych at the Fogg Museum in Boston Massachusetts.

72-74. *SPRING BEGINNINGS* and *WRAPPED IN LEAVES* are about my close German friend, whom I met on a trip to India in 1971, who died in her early fifties.

76-85 MASHIKO. Japan pottery-poems, from *Shards*, Turn of River Press, 2004. I apprenticed in Mashiko, folk pottery village in Japan. At fifty years old, I worked with Hiroshi Kawajri (referred to as *Sensei*, teacher.) His wife, Yumiko Kawajiri, also was a potter. Their three children were Natsumi (then eight); Emi (five); and Teku, (two and a half). Teku now has now taken over his father's kiln and workshop.

My friend Yukako Hayakawa, a Mashiko potter, helped me interview Mashiko potters during the early 1970s. I later wrote my doctoral dissertation at New York University in 1982 on the first generation of folkware in Mashiko. Afterwards, I returned to Mashiko to apprentice with Hiroshi Kawajiri in Mashiko.

78. *RED, NOT YET.* Emi is the Kawajiri's five-year-old child.

APPENDIX

POEMS FROM *A PLAY OF MIRRORS*
A SLICE OF MOONLIGHT
A SKULL FULL OF WORDS
ALICE NEEL AT SEVENTY-SEVEN
DENIAL
DISTRACTION
GARDEN OF EARTHLY DELIGHTS
GIRL IN THE TREE
GIVERNY
IF I'D BEEN THERE THEN
NEAR AND CLOSE
POETRY BONES
THAT BITCH
VISITOR
WITHOUT
WORDLESS

POEMS FROM *A LEAF CALLED SOCRATES*
A LEAF CALLED SOCRATES
ARTICHOKES
BEFORE MOCA OFFICIALLY OPENED
CHINESE SCROLL
DELPHI STILL LIFE
FAMILY PORTRAIT
FIRING MY MUSE
FIRST LOVE
FOGGED IN AT GAY HEAD (retitled: NOT FOGGED IN AT GAY HEAD)
HAWK
IF ONLY
KEY TO TIME
LE DÉJEUNER SUR L'HERBE

MEDUSA
PAINTING THE TRUTH OF LIES
POETRY BONES
REVETMENT
SELF SEEKER
SEPIA ANCESTORS
SURROUNDED BY UNFINISHED WOMEN
TAG SALE CAMEO
THE GARDEN VANISHED
THE WAY
TRAVELING GLASS
WILL VENUS RISE?
WRAPPED IN LEAVES

POEMS FROM *ALZHEIMER'S CHRONICAL*
LIFE CHANGES

POEMS FROM: *A GLANCE BACK*
DA VINCI
DEAD SWAN
LIFE CHANGES (reworked)
NETSUKE
POLIO
SO LITTLE TIME
THAT THAT CANNOT BE FIXED (retitled: THAT THAT CANNOT BE SEEN)

POEMS FROM: SHARDS
COFFEE CEREMONY
MY NEW ROOM
PATINA
NO GOOD AT WORDS
RED? NOT YET
RELIQUARY
RIGHT WRONG ROAD
SA MYO JI TEMPLE

TEN YEARS OF TEA CUPS
THE THREAT OF IMMORTALITY

Made in the USA
Columbia, SC
11 September 2022